MAID MARIAN
AND HER MERRY MEN

THE BEAST OF BOLSOVER

Tony Robinson

Illustrated by Paul Cemmick

BBC Books

This book is based on the BBC TV series
Maid Marian and her Merry Men
by Tony Robinson, produced by Richard Callanan
and directed by David Bell.

Published by BBC Books
a division of BBC Enterprises Ltd
Woodlands, 80 Wood Lane, London W12 0TT

First published 1990
© Tony Robinson 1990
Illustrations © Paul Cemmick 1990

ISBN 0 563 36040 2

Printed and bound in Great Britain by Cooper Clegg Ltd, Tewkesbury
Colour separations by Technik Ltd, Berkhamsted
Cover printed by Richard Clay Ltd, St Ives Plc